Know the Truth ...
The Secret to Life is Within You and Within These Pages

Sandra Crathern

Copyright © 2016 Sandra Crathern

All rights reserved.

ISBN: 1533388156
ISBN-13: 978-1533388155

This book is dedicated to my husband Gary and my three sons Lloyd, Lewis and Elliot for always being there, and for respecting me so much .

CONTENTS

	Foreword	i
1	Examine the Balance in Your Life with my Health Fountain Tool	1
2	The Keys to Great Communication – Live, Love and Laugh	6
3	How to Get, Keep and Nurture Positive Lasting Relationships	12
4	Reduce Stress with my Joy Spirit Level – A Simple Tool to Improve your Life (and that of others around you)	24
5	Enhance Your Wellbeing with Better UTime Management	32
6	Find meditation in a Hectic World with my Peace of Mind Tool	39
7	Meditation: One Simple Step to Amazing Health Benefits	49
8	Simple Steps to Help You Get a Good Night's Sleep	54
9	The Ten Secrets to Happiness	58
10	Afterword, Resources and Further Reading	67

Foreword - Been there, done it!

"One ounce of action is greater than one ton of theory"

Ralph Waldo Emerson

My name is Sandra Crathern, and I am 56. At this very moment I am healthier, fitter and more in control of my life than I have ever been in my entire life. Wow!

I'm writing this book because I would like you to be able to say the same things about yourself. I believe my true purpose on this planet is to help people love and respect themselves as I have been helped to love and respect myself. It's as simple as that.

In order for you to understand a bit more about the journey I have been on, allow me to start at the beginning. My story isn't one of terrible deprivation or desperate circumstances; however, I'm still more like David than Goliath, with a backstory that wasn't conducive to eventually writing a book, or even having a successful career.

I grew up in Crawley in West Sussex, as one of three children. I was fortunate enough to have two very loving parents who adored me. However, they also rather indulged me. If I went on long enough about something, it would happen. With two elder brothers I was the baby of the family, and as sometimes happens in that situation, I was treated differently to them. I was frequently let off the hook for bad behaviour, and given pretty much whatever I wanted. While my brothers might have been severely disciplined for stepping over the line, there were no consequences for me; no one challenged me. I was persistent and insistent in my desires, and so I always got what I wanted. The trouble was, this made me feel different to my brothers - and it wasn't always a good feeling. All of this meant that I had very few boundaries, and from an early age I was used to getting my own way.

Ours was a bilingual household, as my mother is Austrian. My parents used both languages, but when they argued or talked about anything personal to each other, it was in German. I was a naturally curious girl who always wanted to know the answers to everything. My home environment was therefore a bit confusing. Sometimes I felt as if the house was full of mysteries, a sensation which was compounded by the language situation and the fact that I always, always, wanted to know everything that was going on. As a child my parents said I had the gift of the gab - I really could talk for England. But the one thing we didn't talk about, was our feelings.

Looking back at our family eating habits, from a young age I was introduced to a healthy diet consisting of three meals a day of meat, fresh vegetables and fruit. My favourite treats were my Mum's gugelhopf, her snitzel, and a massive, rich, extra eggy version of an English pancake. But they were just that, treats; there's no real excuse in my upbringing for not knowing how to eat healthily.

I was an impatient and headstrong child. My personality combined with the fact that I craved and got an instant fix of whatever I was after, wasn't a good combination. In some ways I feel I was destined for trouble. School was a challenge for me. I could read, but found it very difficult – looking at words gave me a headache, they would jump all over the place. I seemed to find things difficult to grasp and my attention span was limited, so I tended to end up being the class clown. These days such problems would be noticed and addressed, but at that time learning difficulties were much less well understood, and so I received no additional support. The result was that I didn't read a book properly until I was 30, and finally received a diagnosis of moderate dyslexia when I was 38. I believe that if I were at school today I would also be labelled with Attention Deficit Disorder, along with several other labels.

Although I was largely unaware of it at the time, my life really started to unravel when I was about 14. We moved town and I had to change schools, switching from a very informal junior school to a much stricter educational environment. In class, my concentration levels started to deteriorate further.

Interestingly, it was about this time that I started to swap my lunch money for cigarettes. I now know that your brain needs fuel to work, and it is well documented how low blood sugar can adversely affect concentration and moods. This is particularly true for teenagers whose bodies and minds are going through such major changes. It's often a time of emotional change too, so if on top of this you've missed a meal and instead you're smoking a cigarette and eating lots of sugar, you're already compromising your ability to tackle the ups and downs of every day. I started to diet at 12, discovering meal replacement pills, which I would never advise people to use and which are potentially even more problematic for teens.

As my teens went on I went fully off the rails and was pretty much expelled from school, obtaining minimal qualifications. In fact, my careers adviser suggested I would be more suited to borstal (a type of remand centre for unruly kids), due to the attitude I had during those years.

Despite having a problematic attitude, I was always very driven. After school I got a job as an auxiliary in a nursing home. By chance and good luck, one of my co-workers there spotted my potential, and encouraged me to apply to train to become a nurse. I enrolled in Practical State Nursing Training in 1978, having sold myself brilliantly to get onto the training programme. One of my natural born skills, which had been a source of irritation to those around me as a child – the inability to stop talking – came in very handy. Nursing training gave me some much needed discipline. I was guided and encouraged along the way by two key individuals: my ward sister and my then boyfriend, who was soon to become my husband.

My teens and twenties were filled with training, and I got married at the age of 21. My three sons were born in quick succession soon after. However, at the same time I also found drink, slimming clubs, and a combination of diet pills and exercise for my erratic weight gains. I was the classic yo yo dieter, constantly at war with my body. As well as working part time I was managing a busy home. My moods continued to be up and down and I became prone to outbursts of anger, in particular when I was hungry, lonely or tired.

Our home environment changed when my husband went on permanent nightshifts. With no adult company and a busy home life - I was trying to keep the house perfect while looking after three boys as well as holding down a career - I was very lonely a lot of the time. I found it more and more difficult to express my feelings. I was deeply unhappy and so I self-medicated by going out drinking and partying whenever I could.

So my life was stressful, but things got worse because an extra element was thrown into the mix: a lack of self-worth. In some ways the seeds were sown in childhood for my adult feelings of low self-esteem. My parents, like most parents, had the best intentions and did everything out of love. But being very overindulged and getting everything I asked for actually made me feel like I was worth less than other people. I felt insignificant, because I wasn't treated the same way as the others. This coupled with a stubborn, impatient personality full of ego, and the fact that I wasn't able to express my feelings properly, meant that any sense of inner peace was absent from my life.

I reached rock bottom at 37. I was verging on suicidal. I had effectively been in freefall for over 25 years when a friend recommended I read the book "How to Live your Life" by Louise Hay. It was a huge wake up call, which led to me starting to take responsibility for my life. Soon after that I entered the doors of a 12-step recovery programme which saved my life emotionally, mentally, physically and spiritually. I still attend regular meetings and have a daily reprieve from my addictions.

So that's the brief story of my journey, a set of circumstances which have led me to the wonderful, happy, healthy place I'm in today. I developed my unique, tried and tested Innavision tools in response to the challenges I faced in my life, and having trained and studied hard along the way; but you don't have to have as many issues as I did to benefit.

Whatever your situation or background, whatever is happening in your life or whatever set of circumstances prompted you to look at this book – you can make a change. Anyone can make significant improvements to their health and wellbeing, however dire things might seem, or however out of control your life may feel right now. If you read this book and use the Innavision tools, you will feel the benefits. But that's the key: the 'doing'. The American essayist Ralph Waldo Emerson said:

"An ounce of action is worth a ton of theory"

– that is my mantra, and one of the founding principles of Innavision. You can read as much as you like, but unless you actually DO something, it won't have any effect. It sounds obvious and simple, because it is. If you take the right actions, you can achieve peace of mind, a sense of purpose and have more fun. You will be more content, you will be able to deal with stress much better, and your overall wellbeing will improve.

What are you waiting for?

I wish you the very best of luck with your health and wellbeing journey.

Sandra Crathern
Worthing, May 2016

Sandra Crathern

Chapter One

Examine the **Balance** in Your Life with my Health Fountain Tool

"The unexamined life is not worth living."

Socrates

Let's start by looking at your life as a whole. My Health Fountain Tool is a fantastic way of looking holistically at all the areas of your life, and seeing where there might be imbalances. Balance is the key to everything in life; and yours is no different.

There are many different elements which affect your wellbeing, and this tool empowers you to think about these in turn. In doing this, you can really focus on where you feel there are imbalances in your life. Once you have completed working through the tool you can instantly see if your life is balanced.

Find a quiet time and space to do this exercise. On the following page you will find my Health Fountain Tool. Looking at each of the elements of the health fountain in turn, pay attention and careful thought to how happy you are with these areas of your life. Put a ring around one of the numbers on each of the elements to illustrate your level of satisfaction with it. It's best to go with your initial thoughts, and not to readjust them as you go along. Be absolutely honest with yourself here; there's no point in adjusting the odds.

The overall effect indicates how balanced your life is. For example, you may be lucky enough to have a healthy body, and you exercise well and take care of yourself; but if you aren't in a happy relationship, and you don't have much fun in your life, this will have a huge impact on your wellbeing.

KNOW THE TRUTH …

Health Fountain
Respect your health. *From the inside out.*

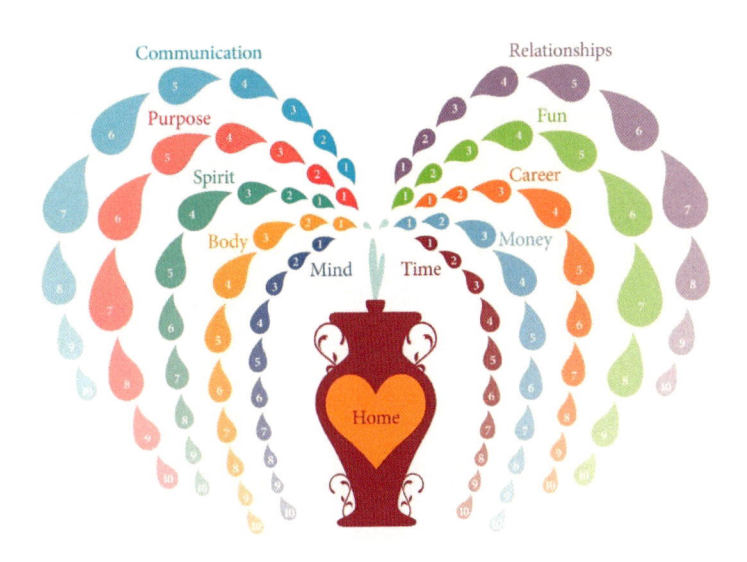

Completing Your Health Fountain

The Health Fountain is a tool to help you take a snapshot of how you feel NOW. Be honest. This is a visual tool to look at the *balance* in your life. It is designed to help you evaluate how you feel.

Using the guide, circle a number from each element of the fountain.

0 = Not very happy, satisfied or content
10 = Very happy, satisfied or content

My Health Fountain Tool is above all a tool of observation. When you look at your Health Fountain, only you can decide whether you feel it is balanced or not. This exercise is about bringing a holistic awareness to what is happening in your life, and to how you are living your life. It should help you identify the elements that you would like to improve. Once you've done this, you can become specific about what you want to change or adjust.

When you have decided what you want to achieve – whether that's small adjustments or major life changes – then you can start to implement your plan. It's about small actions, one at a time, which will move you closer step by step towards your goal.

Know Yourself

Think of any major historical figure, past or present, who you think has (or has had) real personal insight. Don't think too much about what that means right now; just respond to the idea of personal insight – people who really 'know themselves'. Figures such as Mother Theresa, the Dalai Lama, Socrates, the Buddha, and Ghandi are often on that list; individuals who had real, true insight into themselves, and strong self-knowledge. It's not surprising that they can also be looked upon as spiritual figures, or individuals with a strong sense of faith of some sort, religious or not.

A good proportion of people live their lives from day to day, facing each challenge as it comes. The issue with this way of living is that they don't honestly and frankly consider their likes and dislikes, as well as their idiosyncrasies.

Knowing yourself isn't about judging yourself. Instead, it's about **taking responsibility** for where you are and what your life is like at any given time. To succeed in something, you have to invest time in it; this might be a happy marriage or successful career. To achieve the best outcome for each element of your life, you need to invest the time to evaluate it, just as you have to invest time in nurturing a beautiful garden. Of course, your garden will need water and sunshine to grow, but to really flourish it needs careful thought and planning as well as time spent pruning, de-weeding and feeding.

By using the Health Fountain tool and working through these exercises, you will reap the benefits. You'll feel more in control of your life, with greater peace of mind. You'll find that you create more time for yourself, and that includes having more fun. Your energy levels will improve, you'll have more focus, and you'll find it easier to have better self-discipline.

Chapter Two

The Keys to Great **Communication** – Live, Love and Laugh

"The human connection is the key to personal and career success."

Paul J Meyer

It's an easy thing to forget, but communication is a two-way process. This applies both to how you communicate with others, but also how you communicate with yourself. I'll explain a bit more about what that means below.

Body Language

Studies have shown that body language comprises more than half of your communication with others. It is generally clear when you're communicating well with someone and when you're not. However, sometimes it can be so subtle that you may only feel a slight sense of unease.

One basic key element is to look at body language, both yours and the other person's. Observe the other person's body language. Are they smiling? Are you? Are they making eye contact with you? Is their posture relaxed and comfortable – or are they looking stiff, strained, perhaps turning away or angled away from you? How about you? For truly effective communication it is essential that these elements are in place for both parties.

How to be a Good Listener

Listening is a key element of communication. Listening - especially listening well - is a skill in itself, and one which it takes time to learn. There are whole industries and disciplines built upon the skill of listening - that's how important, and complex it is. However, it's relatively easy to learn to be a good listener. You may need to unlearn some bad habits though.

For example, do you ever find yourself pre-empting what the other person is saying, or thinking about what they are about to say next? It's very common to be 'listening' to someone while failing to be fully 'present'. Perhaps you're mentally making a shopping list or running through a particularly difficult part of your day, when you're supposed to be communicating with the person in front of you. You may be listening, but with an agenda; how often have you nodded and smiled while waiting to drop a bombshell or make a difficult request? Perhaps you are trying to listen but are distracted, and are undertaking other tasks at the same time. All of these are examples of not being fully present.

Participating in good listening starts with silence. Repeating small sections of what the other person has said for clarification can be helpful, and can ensure that both parties are in tune with each other.

Don't interrupt, if you can possibly help it. Give the other person time to say what they need to say. Remember, it may take a while, particularly if they are trying to explain something complex or which is emotional for them. And don't automatically offer your opinion unless you are asked to (unless you are in a professional situation where you are required to do so).

Take Responsibility

Take responsibility for how you want to communicate. There is generally more than one choice for how you address a situation.

How effective do you think have been in the past as a communicator? Reflect on a few past situations. Can you think of occasions when you didn't communicate, or listen, as effectively as you could have?

Do you struggle with confrontation? Before tackling difficult situations it's worth thinking about what a positive outcome would look like to you. In every communication situation the aim is a 'win – win', with each person being heard.

Tone of Voice

Less than 10% of communication is made up of the actual words you say! That's great news if you don't have the gift of the gab. The bulk of communication happens through your tone of voice and your body language, not the words you use. For example, have you ever responded to someone to say that you are fine, when your tone and body language clearly show that you are not? We've all done it. And it can be very obvious, even if you're speaking on the telephone.

At least a third of how we communicate is through our tone of voice. Even when your body language is open and relaxed, if your tone of voice is raised or lowered this will have an impact on what you are saying. It is important to become aware of your own voice. If you are feeling under pressure this can affect your tone of voice, with the effect that you can come across as angry or irritated.

It is important to ensure that you not only speak slowly, but that the other person can hear you. Aim to speak with a soft but firm tone.

Being Present

Being present isn't only about listening and focussing on the other person; it's also about recognising how you feel. The current buzzword for being present is Mindfulness, a simple explanation of which is that it's a way of focussing the mind and breath by being fully in the present moment. It also refers to awareness. In practising Mindfulness, whatever you're doing – whether that's walking, talking, or working - you need to practise being really present. People who meditate in a quiet peaceful space with their eyes closed often feel the benefits of just *being* instead of *doing.*

You can do this right now. Take a minute to notice how you are feeling. Are you angry? Frustrated? Lonely? Fearful? Resentful? Any feelings you have will make a difference to how you respond to situations, so it is important to be able to recognise them. Owning how you feel is about being really honest and congruent, two areas which play a large part in good communication. Be authentic; allow yourself to be who you really are.

Chapter Three

How to Get, Keep and Nurture Positive Lasting **Relationships**

"You've got to love yourself first, and until you value yourself enough to know that, you can't really have a healthy relationship."

Jennifer Lopez

Getting to Know Yourself

Getting to know yourself properly is fundamental to any relationship. If you don't know or can't decide what you need as a person, then you won't be able to communicate that to anyone else. You need to have a good and positive relationship with yourself before being able to get into a good and positive relationship with anyone else. It's simple really: loving and respecting ourselves allows us to love and respect another.

Let's start with a few questions. Fill out the boxes below as honestly as you can. Be brief with your answers and *try not to overthink them too much:*

Write down your own values, and what values you respect in a relationship (for example loyalty, authenticity, trust, honesty and so on)

What types of relationships do you attract, or have you had in the past?

Is your current relationship, or lack of a current relationship, working for you?

> Do you seem to attract the same types of relationships?

> Did any past relationships work for you? If not, why not?

> What do you want from a relationship?

Hindsight is a great tool when we reach the end of a relationship, but the challenge is trying to avoid looking back and saying to ourselves, if only…

It is worth knowing you can have a great relationship whether you are at the beginning, middle or end of it. Even after many years it is still possible to improve things and achieve a deeper and more meaningful relationship.

Now you've done some soul-searching, what's next? One of the first things you can do to move towards better relationships is to take care of yourself. The two main areas to focus on here are **diet** and **rest.**

From a medical point of view, it is well known that if your blood sugars are erratic and unstable, it will negatively affect your mood, concentration and focus. One of the main things which affects our blood sugars is our diet. Eating too much sugar or processed food, having erratic mealtimes or missing mealtimes altogether will have consequences that affect your day-to-day ability to get on with your life. Ultimately these patterns will create a series of mental and physical knock-on effects; these may include disrupted sleep, low moods, anxiety and depression as well as stomach-related ailments, from IBS to stomach ulcers. None of these symptoms are going to help you function in a healthy relationship.

Regular, healthy, fresh meals, eaten sitting down at a table at a regular time of day allows us to be more in control of our diet. This in turn balances our blood sugars which enables our moods to be more stable, thus making a significant contribution towards any healthy, happy, relationship.

As human beings we all need to have sufficient rest. The amount of rest we need differs from person to person; however, putting ourselves first, knowing when to stop and taking the rest we need must be a priority.

Take responsibility for your body and how you feel – and good relationships will flow out from that healthy start.

Keeping it Real

People get married, have a beautiful wedding, spend money on a lovely honeymoon and are full of the best intentions of enjoying a beautiful life together ever after. It's the fairy tale we're all sold in early childhood. The problem is, with such high expectations, we're almost setting ourselves up for failure before we even really get started.

One of the biggest problems in relationships is a lack of effective communication. As soon as possible in any relationship, and certainly before marriage, make sure you're both regularly taking time away from phones, computers and other electronic forms of interference, to make time for simply **talking**.

It's interesting that in the initial stages of a relationship, talking doesn't seem to be a problem. Often those heady early days of a relationship are characterised by a lot of finding out about each other and talking late into the night. However, this won't always be the case. Several years into a relationship, when you are both used to each other, you've excavated all the ins and outs of each other's personalities, you may have got married or had children, your jobs, responsibilities and demands have changed – that's when it becomes really important to stay connected.

How can you do this? Here are a few suggestions:

- Every week make it a priority to **effectively communicate** with each other. Ideally this should happen every day for at least 10 minutes – or if that's not possible, then for a dedicated couple of hours each week as a minimum. See the previous chapter The Keys to Great Communication to make sure you're doing it properly! To recap, that means *actively* listening, not multi-tasking at the same time, and using open body language and eye contact.

- **Keeping it real** is also about accepting that no-one is going to be 100% perfect in every relationship. Everyone has their off-days.

- **Focus on the positive** as much as possible. Dwelling on negatives does nobody any good.

- **Make time to enjoy each other's company.** This can be something as simple as walking together to get the paper at the weekend, to as extravagant as a special weekend away, just the two of you. It doesn't matter what you do, or how much it costs, as long as you both enjoy it.

- **It's okay to disagree.** It would be a very dull world if we all had the same opinions on things, or we all wanted the same things. It's how you deal with the disagreement that matters.

- **Deal with difficulties.** It is important not to ignore our feelings, but stick with the facts. Work towards resolution by focussing on the solution rather than the problem.

- **Have a laugh.** When we laugh the body the body releases endorphins, which are the body's natural feel good chemicals. Endorphins promote an overall sense of wellbeing, as well as being natural pain relievers and stress busters.

Learning to say NO – Setting Boundaries

This is one of the most difficult things to do in a relationship. Saying no is often associated with feelings of guilt, fear and unworthiness, and goes against some people's desire for 'people pleasing'. Early relationships can develop in a haze of pink fluffy clouds, with each party being considerate and making compromises; but as time goes on it is important to develop healthy boundaries as you settle into long-term routines.

Very often when one party says 'No' in a relationship, it's hard for that person to deal with the effect. It is normal not to want conflict. We are by nature comfort-seekers, but in reality, we all need to occasionally experience discomfort at some level, and learn how to deal with it. It is ironic that most of us would expect others to be honest in a relationship, but when faced with the same challenge we may find it difficult to do. We must therefore experience the discomfort of being completely honest in order to move towards a more positive and open relationship. With practice comes ease.

It is also important to remember that we don't always have to give a reason for our decisions, just a simple answer will do. Just make sure that your answer is clear and concise and given with confidence.

Not being respected by a partner is a well-voiced complaint. If you don't feel respected then it's unlikely that you're going to be comfortable saying 'no' sometimes. Spending time getting to know yourself is a good transition towards being able to say 'No' confidently, as you will get to know what you do and don't need and want.

Self-respect and self-confidence are the building blocks for a happy relationship. The healthier and more clearly defined the boundaries within a relationship are, the more likely it is you will be respected within that relationship. Those with low self-confidence and self-respect are often greeted with such.

Learning to say no is a process. It won't happen overnight. The first time you say 'No', set a new boundary or ask for something you wouldn't have previously - you're stepping outside your comfort zone. You may have heard the saying 'the definition of madness is repeating the same behaviour and expecting a different result'. The only person you can change is yourself, so if you would like a different relationship, **you** have to make the first move.

Honesty can be very difficult if you are used to 'people pleasing' and saying what you believe someone wants to hear. Once you have decided to become more honest you will need determination and commitment to keep focussed. The internal commitment needed to take on and deal with another person's negative responses shouldn't be underestimated; it takes real bravery to have the ability to accept another person's honest feelings, even and especially when they differ from your own. Most people change their behaviour when they have just about reached crisis point, when they are truly fed up with unhappy and unhealthy recurring patterns. To change these patterns and break the cycle, you need to focus first on what change would look like, and what it would be like to make a change.

Now ask yourself a few more questions. Perhaps by now you may be feeling clearer about your relationships than at the beginning of the chapter.

Are you willing to make changes?

Are you willing to evaluate the part that you play in negative behaviour?

Have you noticed any positive relationship role models around you? What is good about those relationships?

What do they do differently to you?

What do you want in your relationship?

Take responsibility for yourself, and don't play the blame game. It doesn't get you anywhere in the long run.

When you are able to express your own needs calmly you will be able to approach someone else with your needs. It is a step-by-step process; changing the habits of a lifetime won't happen overnight. All relationships are a work-in-progress; once you start it can seem like an uphill journey, but it will only get easier.

Chapter Four

Reduce **Stress** with my Joy Spirit Level – A Simple Tool to Improve your Life (and that of others around you)

"The greatest weapon against stress is our ability to choose one thought over another."

William James

Let me ask you a question. Have you ever reacted, when you wish you had simply *responded?* It's something most of us do from time to time. In this chapter I'm going to introduce you to my Joy Spirit

Level, an incredibly useful tool for helping you to gain self-control.

In my mid to late twenties, with three children aged four and under, I was working part-time as a nurse in a GP Practice, (ironically) often giving advice on a healthy, work-life balance. I ran a tight ship at home, washing, cooking, ironing and cleaning. Organising was my best asset. You could have called me Super Woman - but underneath I never seemed to have enough time or energy, and found myself emotionally exhausted and behaving erratically with angry outbursts.

By slowing down and learning how to manage my life more realistically I became more aware of the six areas I needed to address on a daily basis, and was able to notice when I needed to ask for help. Using this tool profoundly changed my life and ultimate wellbeing.

Most of us have experienced a situation where we wish we had responded in a different way. Using my Joy Spirit Level tool (overleaf) will help you break down your responses into tiny steps, allowing you to regain control over your emotions, and enabling you to communicate clearly and effectively the next time you're in a stressful situation.

Innavision

1	2	3	4	5	6
Stop	**Address Needs**	**Energy Level**	**Prioritise**	**Feelings**	**Action**
Breath Think Connect	Water Food Rest	1-10	Time Realistic	Anxiety Fear Worry	Acceptance Choices

Joy Spirit Level
Respect your health. From the inside out.

Stop, Breathe, Think and Connect

Other than in an emergency situation such as a fire or road traffic accident, where you are unable to override your natural instincts, when faced with a difficult situation it is important to remember that *you generally always have time to make a choice.* It is possible to create time between stimulus and response. This is something that takes practice.

You need to start by identifying the stimulus - which could be a person, place or object - and then STOP. Take a deep breath and make some time to think. The stimulus is the 'trigger' or cause for your (over)reaction.

Address Your Needs

Are you fed and watered? If you haven't eaten or drunk anything for a number of hours it can distort your sense of reality. Eating regularly keeps your blood sugar levels consistent. Making the time for your body's basic needs is essential. Whenever possible, stay away from unnatural, highly processed and fast foods as they are not good sources of nutrition.

Listen to Your Body

Thinking about your energy levels and whether or not you have eaten or are rested, is taking time to listen to your body. It is important to look at both your feelings and emotions as well as your physical needs to truly understand yourself and what your body is telling you.

How would you describe your energy levels? Can you give them a score from 0 – 10, where 0 is no energy at all, and 10 is feeling fully energised, ready for anything?

Part of evaluating your energy levels can be done by asking yourself, 'How tired am I? How motivated am I?' If your energy levels are low, you are much more likely to overreact to a stimulus. Think about the situation you are in; if you don't have to respond immediately, it could be helpful to take time to think about the best way to deal with it. The higher your energy levels are, the better you will be equipped to deal with stressful situations. Higher energy levels generally bring greater motivation and commitment to finding solutions.

Prioritise Your Time – What is Realistic?

The next step is to prioritise. What has to be addressed now, and what can be addressed later? Once you've decided the order of priority, then you can prioritise your responses to the situation. It may be that some issues can be addressed when you are not tired, hungry, or late for work.

Most people have unrealistic expectations of themselves and others. Is this the case for you? If you are not feeling your 100% best, your energy levels are low, or you are hungry, what is the correct course of action to take now?

Take some time to evaluate your priorities. Whose

responsibility is it? Can someone help you? Are you being realistic about what you expect from others?

If you are in a stressful situation take some time to clarify the facts; not doing so may affect your perception of reality. Being realistic about a situation and responding effectively can often simply be down to communication.

Notice how the Stimulus Makes you Feel

As I said above, the stimulus is the 'trigger' or cause for your overreaction. This could be a person, place, occasion, event, sound – there are many possible stimuli and everyone's stress points are different. Do you feel angry, resentful, frustrated, lonely, tired, bored, scared, or fearful? Are you hungry?

Actions, Choices and Acceptance

Ideally, and if the situation allows, write down what choices there are, or at least take time to think about them. When you focus on the solution, the solution gets bigger. And conversely, when you focus on the problem, the problem gets bigger.

If you have a set of choices, think each one through

to the end. Are you happy with the outcome? You can always add something to a course of action, but you cannot take it away.

At times you may find there are not many choices and you have to accept the situation as it is, and let go.

In Conclusion

Often people say they are too busy to take the time to think about how they are feeling, or whether they are rested and so on. However, if you practise these skills, the better the results become and the less likely you are to make irrational choices and responses. The choices you make will come to be based on pure information, as well as taking into account your feelings, emotions and energy levels.

Chapter Five

Enhance Your Wellbeing with Better **UTime Management**

"Until we can manage time, we can manage

nothing else"

Peter Drucker

I often hear people saying, "I don't have time". To that I say, we all have 24 hours in each day, and it is your choice what you put in that 24 hours.

If that sounds simple, it's because it is. This chapter is about how managing your time to achieve the best results will dramatically enhance your life and wellbeing.

Making time for ourselves can very often be the last on our list of priorities, with other commitments taking precedence. Family, work, friends, busy schedules and financial affairs all seem to come higher up the list. Most people are apparently programmed to attend to these 'things' before 'themselves'.

This kind of behaviour is often ingrained in our thinking as it has been learnt from a very young age. We are pre-programmed this way, having often witnessed it in the actions of our parents. We are often brought up to put others before ourselves and to think about what we can do for others.

Turning this around and putting ourselves first tends to come with negative feelings such as guilt, shame, feelings of selfishness, and uneasiness. This can be very hard to tackle. But the amazing thing about putting yourself first and making time for yourself, is the phenomenal benefits you reap.

What you may be unaware of is the physical and mental impact of constantly putting other people and other things first. At some level, resentment builds up. Exhaustion and stress, high blood pressure, anxiety, sleep disorders and burnout are some of the symptoms people experience.

It's very common for people presenting at the GP's surgery with stress-related ailments to be advised to rest well, learn to say 'no' and put themselves first. We are often excellent at giving advice to our children, friends and family, suggesting they slow down and put themselves first - but can't seem to manage it ourselves. Often the reality is we find it impossible to do - we don't know how to, or where to start.

UTime management is not about planning so much that your diary is crammed with more and more things to squeeze into your day. It is much more about taking things out of your diary, planning in time for yourself, creating holistic space and time for yourself. Above all, it is about balance.

The first thing to be aware of is that putting yourself first, and putting your health first, sit together. Life can be easy to get caught up in, and it takes real self-discipline to create time for ourselves. Planning each day around a regular framework may be beneficial, with primary consideration given to how long each task should realistically take. Within this framework you must block out time for eating unprocessed foods, sat down, at a table, without distraction. It is also worth considering the benefits of giving your mind a break from the TV, radio, emails and mobile phones - and just focussing on doing one task at a time.

Multi-tasking is a contributing factor towards anxiety. This is because if you multi-task, you're not fully present for any of the tasks in hand. Multi-tasking is sadly en-vogue at the moment. Many people strive to multi-task more effectively, and efficiently, to demonstrate their skills and aptitude. Employers seek to endorse a multi-tasking culture through their performance reviews, and with computer programmes designed to enable you to switch effortlessly from one unfinished task to the next.

A regular framework for your day, encompassing the key tasks you need to set aside time for, should be your starting point. You need to include three meals a day, winding down before bed, with some quiet time. Set aside time in your day to complete one task at a time. Make sure you have some time for fun and relaxation, without over-committing yourself.

In order to start to break repetitive cycles including multi-tasking, poor diet and eating habits, late nights, rushing around and putting others before yourself, the first steps might be to consider the following questions:

Do you feel you contented with your life?
Do you feel calm and in control most of the time?
Do you feel rested and energised after a night's sleep?
Are you at a normal, healthy body weight?
Do you want to change?

If you are answering 'no' to most of the above, now is the time to make changes. Here's where to start.

In order to put yourself first you need to:

Believe you are worth it

Give yourself permission

Start with a small change

Take responsibility

Decide what specifically you want / try to achieve

Honour your commitments to yourself,

equal to commitments to others

The answers will be different for every one of you - but it's often the simplest changes which can have the greatest impact. For example, one client's light bulb moment came when they started setting personal appointments first, and then scheduled work appointments around those personal appointments. This shift in priorities instantly allowed that person to take back control of their life.

If you are able to put yourself first, the knock-on effect of looking after yourself properly directly relates to how much energy and capacity you have for looking after others. Fulfilling your personal needs allows you to be more available to others.

If you are enjoying life and having fun, you are well

rested, have eaten healthily and regularly, you are being mindful with your time, and are avoiding situations which may cause you anxiety and stress - you will inevitably feel calmer, more relaxed, happier, more in control of your life and more content. The harsh reality is, being a martyr doesn't serve anyone, least of all yourself.

Remember my favourite quote: "One OUNCE of action is greater than one TON of theory" – Ralph Waldo Emerson. Put one small change in place today, and you will start reaping the benefits.

Chapter Six

Find **Peace** in a Hectic World with my Peace of Mind Tool

"Be the change you want to see in the world."

Mahatma Gandhi

I created the Peace of Mind tool, which you will see in a few pages' time, to help you look at and think about the different elements of your mind. If you respect all these different elements you will gain greater peace of mind, and you will be empowered to recognise any contributing factors that can disturb your mind's peace. Once you are able to identify these factors it will give you a clearer picture of what you need to change.

There are eight elements within the Peace of Mind tool. All are equally important. The higher the percentage of your attention you can apply to each of the elements, the greater your peace of mind will be.

People have an illusion that peace is an external force. We may say *'If my kids would just shut up'*, *'If my husband would help more'*, *'If my manager would leave me alone'* - only then would I have more peace of mind.

This tool actively encourages you to **take responsibility** for yourself and your actions, and will help you to avoid engaging in the 'blame game'.

Before you do the exercise, let's look at all the elements of the Peace of Mind Tool in turn.

Authenticity

This is about being real. It is about being true to yourself. Very often people don't want to be authentic because they don't want to offend someone, they feel uncomfortable or they just don't like to say what they feel or really mean.

There are many reasons you might not want to be

authentic. Fear of confrontation, and a tendency towards people-pleasing are two common reasons, but there are many others. Sometimes it is easier to just 'go with the flow'. It is worth taking into consideration that these habits can be learnt behaviour; they're not always a conscious choice. We may be following the examples we have grown up with.

Self-Respect

Many of us believe we respect ourselves, but ask yourself the following questions:

- Are you eating healthily, getting to bed on time and making healthy lifestyle choices?
- Do you have good self-esteem?
- Do you respect your own feelings, without ignoring them or feeling guilty about them?
- Are your expectations of yourself too high?
- Do you have good boundaries? Are you comfortable in saying 'No'?
- Are you really respecting yourself and taking care of yourself, as you would advise others to?

If you can move towards a greater, more authentic

state of self-respect, you will find it has a massive knock-on effect in terms of how others around you also respect you.

Purpose and Spirit

The biggest question you can be asked, or ask yourself is 'What is your **purpose**'? Research has shown that a high proportion of people suffering from depression don't feel they have a purpose.

Feeling you have a purpose is not always directly linked to being in work, or earning a substantial income. Having a purpose, for some people, is having a family. For others it may be engaging in charitable activities, or running their own business. The purpose itself is not important, it's the belief that you have a purpose and a reason to enjoy each day.

What do you understand by the word **spirit**? Do you have faith in some kind of higher power? If you do, again research shows that you are more likely to recover from illness quicker and encounter fewer stress-related symptoms. Eastern cultures, for thousands of years, have known and believed that a person is made up of mind, body and spirit. This is true for faiths from all over the world, from Buddhism to Christianity and many more.

Maybe your sense of spirit isn't directly linked to any one faith. Do you believe we came from nowhere to return to nowhere - or is that place somewhere within you? This is a powerful concept, a belief in a power greater than yourself. For some, their sense of spirit is the power they feel inside that keeps them going.

Loyalty

Do you consider yourself a loyal person? This isn't about the most obvious notion of loyalty, of being loyal to your partner. Loyalty isn't just about marriage or commitment; it is about being loyal throughout your life - to your colleagues, your boss, your friends and family. And, to yourself. Loyalty towards yourself can be difficult to assess because you are the only real judge. Think about your loyalties towards your own values and beliefs. Are you honouring the commitments you make to yourself as well others?

Honesty

Like loyalty, this element goes further than ideas about truth and lies, or the question about whether you'd hand in the £5 you found in the street. It's about having a sense of honesty throughout your life. Ask yourself questions like:

- Do you leave the office an hour earlier when you should still be at work, or do you 'borrow' the photocopier paper?
- Are you honest about how you feel?
- Are you honest to yourself as well as others?

Integrity

Integrity can be hard to define. Thinking about how much integrity you have covers everything from your sense of honesty and honour, your principles, ethics and morals, a sense of righteousness, virtue, decency, fairness, as well as scrupulousness, sincerity, truthfulness and trustworthiness. In order to help you evaluate whether or not you possess a level of integrity, consider the following questions:

- Are you a reliable person?
- Do you honour your commitments (to yourself as well as others)?
- Do you have good morals, values and ethical principles which you adhere to?

Many elements covered in this book overlap; it is important to remember that they all make up part of the bigger picture of your general health and wellbeing.

How to use the Peace of Mind Tool

Once you have been able to spend some time considering these elements, put a percentage next to each of them that represents how 'Authentic' or 'Loyal' you feel you are. This exercise isn't a game to achieve 100%; however, the higher the percentage you can attain in each of these elements, the greater your peace of mind will be.

If your mind isn't peaceful you are more likely to feel anxious, agitated, un-motivated, tired, frustrated and at times unable to control your emotions. You may find yourself lacking in self-discipline, suffering from the ability to focus, as well as being easily distractible. You will also be less able to give your time and attention to others, which will affect you and your relationships at home and at work as well as with yourself.

KNOW THE TRUTH …

Peace/Piece of Mind
Respect your health. *From the inside out.*

- Purpose
- Spirituality
- Loyalty
- Credibility
- Integrity
- Authenticity
- Self Respect
- Honesty

Peace of Mind Tool

Carefully think about each of the above elements and write down as a percentage a representative of how you feel you are in each, as an example, I am 85% 'Authentic' or 95% 'Loyal'.

The benefits of greater peace of mind include:

- Improved sleep quality
- Reduced blood pressure
- Improved relationships, happier, healthier
- A greater sense of relaxation
- A feeling of being lighter in yourself and having more fun
- A general sense of all round healthier wellbeing

To increase your peace of mind you need to be really honest with yourself. Over time you should try to increase the percentage you apportion to each element of the Peace of Mind Tool. This will require taking action; considering your feelings in depth, and evaluating your conduct in relation to each of the elements. With time and practice you'll find you can act differently - more authentically, more honestly, with greater integrity and so on across all the elements of the Peace of Mind Tool.

If you don't feel that you have a certain level of peace of mind most of the time, then you need to reassess the elements. It is fair to say that usually one or more of them will be out of alignment. If you are able to increase your percentage ratings you will over time have greater peace of mind.

Chapter Seven

Meditation: One Simple Step to Amazing Health Benefits

"Where there is peace and meditation there is neither anxiety or doubt."

St Francis de Sales

Mindful meditation is very much 'en vogue' at the moment; in many ways it's the wellbeing buzzword of the decade. In fact, meditation is an ancient practice which modern science has proven to have multiple benefits. These include:

- Lower blood pressure
- Reduced anxiety
- A slowing down of the aging process

- Relaxation of the nervous system
- Increased productivity
- Increased peace of mind and happiness

Best of all, meditation is completely FREE! Anyone can do it, anytime, anywhere, with no specialist equipment. Meditation also helps us to connect with our bodies, strengthening our relationships with ourselves. Practising regular mindful meditation allows us to find stillness in an otherwise busy, stressful world.

It is interesting to note that most religions practise some form of meditation, whether or not it's called meditation; Buddhism, Christianity and Hinduism for starters. A quick glance at the Internet will show you that there are around 23 different types of meditation, some with fancy names such as Transcendental Meditation and Zen Meditation. One of my key aims when I work with clients is to make things as simple as possible, and to maximise results as much as possible. So how do you get started, and what do you need to do?

The hardest thing about meditation is that you need to do absolutely nothing - which can be difficult to comprehend. Our brains tend to be on constant alert and we are often programmed to cram as much action as possible into each day.

In contrast, I would suggest starting with just a few minutes of being quiet. Then:

- Find a nice space where you won't be disturbed by the phone or other people.
- Sit in a warm comfortable place, without distractions. No smartphones, headphones, radios or TV. Just you.
- Allow yourself to close your eyes. Begin to focus on your breathing, slowly allowing yourself to have longer breaths out.
- The key to meditation is simply, slowing down. Concentrate on your breathing, as well as really noticing and focusing on what you are doing right now.

The purpose of mindful meditation is to bring you back to the present moment. As your thoughts drift, gently allow yourself to connect again with your breathing and the stillness around you. The aim of meditation is to bring you to the present moment.

Initially meditation can be a very difficult thing to practise, especially if your brain is constantly active, with your 'to-do' list jumping into your head, or your mind wandering in its own direction.

Mindfulness is about bringing your mind back to the here and now, just the present moment.

The past has gone, and only lessons learnt from it are worth hanging onto. Projecting into the future is pointless, and a waste of time and energy. So much anxiety and stress comes from worrying about things which have already happened which we have no control over, or thinking about future events which may never happen.

The wonderful thing about making time to be still and quiet and connect with our bodies, is that an almost magical feeling of calmness, control and choice falls into place.

Like any new pursuit, the only way to benefit from meditation's full potential is to practise. Therefore, it is important to make a commitment to yourself to include regular meditation in your daily routine.

Once you're practising regular mindful meditation you'll start to notice that when stressful moments arrive, which we all experience on more or less a daily basis, simply adopting a quiet posture, slowing down your breathing and relaxing your body will be enormously empowering, enabling you to deal with the situation much better. Meditation will become a tool you can use each and every day, not only in the time you set aside to practise.

In addition to the benefits outlined above, mindful meditation can also help with recurrent depression, anxiety disorders, addictive behaviour, stress, chronic pain, chronic fatigue syndrome, insomnia and other mental health problems.

There are many ways in which you can learn more about this powerful activity, from researching the Internet, buying special guided meditation CDs or taking part in one of the many classes available to you in your local community.

Chapter Eight
Simple Steps to Help You Get a Good Night's **Sleep**

"Early to bed, and early to rise, makes a man healthy, wealthy and wise."

Benjamin Franklin

If you are a parent, or have ever looked after a baby, take a moment to consider how you might approach settling the baby to sleep. I expect that there are lots of factors that you would think about. A quiet, warm, aired environment; a comfortable bed, with the appropriate bedding for the surrounding environment and season; low or no lighting.

Now think about **your** sleeping environment; does it match up with that of the (theoretical) baby's? It is useful to pay attention to the details of getting ourselves to bed, and ensuring that our sleeping conditions are conducive to a good night's sleep. These conditions are very basic, but are often forgotten, and this should be your starting point.

I want to reiterate here that many of the solutions you will find in this book, including in this chapter, involve addressing basic, fundamental issues. In my experience the fundamentals have often been neglected through the development of bad habits or learnt behaviour. If you are suffering from more complex physical or mental conditions you must address these first, to give yourself the best chance of a positive outcome for any situation.

Devise a personal bedtime routine for yourself which includes a decent period of time to 'wind down' and prepare for sleep. You should leave sufficient time between eating and sleeping, not going to bed too soon after eating a heavy meal.

You may like to take a bath or shower. Your bedtime routine may be a good time to practise some mindful meditation (see the previous chapter), or to listen to a relaxation CD which can set the right atmosphere. For some, practising their faith and/or praying can play a part in a bedtime routine, which can lead to greater relaxation and relief of anxiety.

Interestingly there is research to suggest you should avoid listening to negative news before going to bed, as this may affect your unconscious mind. It's a good idea to retire to bed early and simply rest, before attempting sleep. Often writing a to-do list for the next day can unburden your mind and relieve anxiety. Keep a pad and pen by the bedside, for writing down restless or prolonged thoughts at bedtime or during the night.

Make sure you allow enough time to sleep; most people need somewhere in the region of 6 to 8 hours. In addition, you may find you sleep better in an attractive, tidy environment, so prioritise making your bedroom as pleasant as it can be.

To avoid harbouring negativity overnight you may need to make time to digest, write down or discuss thoughts and feelings. Take care not to approach controversial or sensitive subjects to close to bedtime, as often you may be tired at that time of day, and there may not be 'enough time' to discuss matters properly. Chapters Two and Four on Communication and Stress respectively have some great tools and tips that can be applied to the bedtime routine.

Visualisation can be an extremely useful tool to aid restful sleep. During your last thoughts before you drop off, take some time to visualise yourself in a peaceful place, imagining yourself waking up refreshed and re-energised.

To get a good night's sleep, try to avoid:

- Smoking
- Alcohol
- High fat and sugary foods
- Caffeine
- Dwelling on the past
- Focussing on the future
- Being excessively over- or underweight
- Drinking too much fluid close to bedtime
- Reading or playing on your smartphone or tablet close to bedtime
- Arguing before bed / entering into confrontational or controversial conversation
- Watching or reading highly emotive or disturbing material, programmes or films
- Reinforcing bad night habits, such as getting up, eating or drinking, or working.

If you are still suffering with sleeping problems you may need to consider medical help, counselling or coaching as a form of support. Don't suffer alone; there is a lot of assistance out there.

Chapter Nine

The Ten Secrets to **Happiness**

"He who lives in harmony with himself lives in harmony with the universe."

Marcus Aurelius

In this final chapter I'm going to share with you the ten secrets to happiness. They are all within your grasp.

1. Slow Down

Less haste, less speed!

Slowing down can be very difficult to do. We are living in an age of multi-tasking, constantly being asked to do more than one thing at a time. However, completing one task properly before moving onto the next can be very rewarding. What's more, you are less likely to make mistakes when in a hurry.

2. Eat Healthily

One of the best, and simplest things you can do for your health is to eat (ideally) fresh, unprocessed foods. Simple, natural, unprocessed foods are the best. Eat them regularly, whilst sat down at a table. It is so important to make time for regular meals throughout the day.

Eating healthily is a very important part of achieving balance in your life, but contrary to many beliefs it is not the only element in a healthy lifestyle and should be addressed alongside other elements to achieve the correct balance. A healthy body, however, underpins all aspects of your life and without one true happiness will be harder to find.

Eating is a fundamental part of your life; therefore, careful consideration needs to be given to how and when you eat. As mentioned, eating regularly whilst sat down at a table, and allowing yourself enough time to eat properly without rushing, will pay dividends. Eating away from distractions will give you time in your day to refocus and energise, which will help you be more productive overall.

3. Be Authentic

Authenticity is really about being yourself; about showing and sharing your core values and beliefs. It's OK to use the 'I' word. Let people know who you are. Let others know how you feel.

Some people find it difficult to show who they are as they are fearful of upsetting others. From a young age many of us are taught to bury our feelings and 'fit in'. Sometimes this can contribute to a habit of burying our feelings, but it can also result in other feelings such as resentment, anger and frustration.

These types of feelings create dis-ease – that's to say, 'disease'. They can contribute to various medical problems ranging from anxiety and depression to deep-rooted anger issues as well as strokes, high blood pressure and/or high cholesterol.

The majority of people strive towards being authentic, and would like nothing more than to be themselves. But in a world of judgement and high expectations it is easy to be swept along and lose our own identity at the expense of 'fitting in' and being accepted.

4. Put Yourself First

The hardest thing to do can be to put yourself first. This means listening to your body and responding appropriately. Many of us are socially and behaviourally conditioned to put others before ourselves, and this can be something we have grown up with. And because this is an expectation developed by wider society, if you put yourself first you may feel that you're criticised by others, as it can be seen as being selfish.

A good example of why it's vital to put yourself first comes from the safety demonstration before a flight, which most of us will have sat through. The flight attendant tells you to place the oxygen mask on yourself before trying to help others. This clearly demonstrates that unless you take care of yourself, you will not be as fit to take care of others.

There is a positive domino effect which comes from putting yourself first. When you have had the time to look after your own needs, you will have more energy and resources to give to others when you need to.

5. Listen to your body

Are you hungry? Tired? Do you need a rest?

We spend far too much time pushing ourselves and our expectations are too high. If you were to give yourself some advice what would it be?

Slow down! Give yourself a break! Take care of yourself!

What you can do when you are 20 years old is very different from what you can do when you are 50. You need to be realistic in what you expect from yourself. In order to do this, take some time to stop and just listen to your body; recognise what it is telling you to do.

6. Have Some Fun

Fun can be defined as enjoyment, amusement, or light-hearted pleasure. People often have fun when they are with others. Make time to plan something which you really enjoy.

It has been mentioned that the average four year old laughs 300 times a day - a 40 year old, only four. But we should all try to laugh more – it's so good for you! Laughing releases very powerful 'feel good' endorphins in your body. You physically take in more oxygen by opening up your lungs, introducing more oxygen to your bloodstream. Laughing is good for your health. Laughter relaxes the whole body. A good, hearty laugh relieves physical tension and stress, leaving your muscles relaxed and boosts the immune system.

It can be all too easy to eliminate things you enjoy from your life because so many other things can take priority. Having fun has its place in a healthy lifestyle and it is important to prioritise it and make time for it.

7. Get Into Nature

Go for a walk, and fill your lungs with fresh air. It's almost impossible not to feel a little bit better, straightaway. A good source of Vitamin D comes from sunlight, and exposing your skin to the sun enhances your mood and energy. Generally, a little bit of sun exposure is linked to a better mood. But don't catch too much!

When we walk outside in the countryside it can have a calming effect on our nervous system. Through experiencing the freedom of the outdoors, and taking time to notice the beauty of nature and the outdoors, we can find a real sense of peace and connection to the world. It helps us to feel that we are a part of nature and to see the bigger picture.

8. Find a Sense of Spirituality

There are many aspects of a person which need to work together harmoniously to create the right balance, and a sense of spirituality is one of them. There is evidence that spirituality and religion are pre-historic, and have been practised for several millennia. Some kind of religion has been practised in every society we have evidence of.

The Impact of Spirituality Upon Mental Health Report [1] created by the Mental Health Foundation in 2006 notes that depression is the most common mental health problem in the UK. There are approximately 121 million people worldwide affected by depression.

If you are open to exploring a sense of spirituality, close your eyes for a period of time and just start to explore within yourself. Try to discover what spirituality means to you. People who have a sense

---

[1] The full report is available at https://www.mentalhealth.org.uk/sites/default/files/impact-spirituality.pdf.

of spirituality report feeling calmer, more comforted, happier, peaceful, and more content.

If you don't have any faith and you are open to exploring spirituality, you might ask yourself how to find a belief in or sense of something bigger than yourself, of a greater meaning to life and our purpose here. Those without a deeper belief in something other than themselves often feel something is missing. Is this how you feel?

It can often take a while to find what you are looking for. It may just be helpful to meditate and focus on your thoughts, leaving your mind open for suggestion.

9. Live in the Present

Yesterday is history and tomorrow is a mystery. We only really have NOW. This is a common mantra within 12-step programmes, and for good reason.

You cannot change the past; its main benefit is to learn from it. Planning is important, but the reality is that the future hasn't yet arrived. Fully living in the present moment takes discipline. It requires some practice to control your thoughts, preventing your mind getting caught up in feelings from the past and worries about the future.

To achieve balance and to gain as much enjoyment as we can we must live in the present - not worrying about the past, or indeed the future.

10. Ask for Help

It's not always easy to achieve everything you desire on your own, and at times it is important to ask for help. Asking for help can be one of the most difficult things to do. If you have tried on your own and don't feel you have succeeded as well as you would have liked, it is even more important to remember that there really is so much help available to you. Think about asking friends, family, other relatives, doctors, coaches, counsellors, support and networking groups.

If you need help, then take the first step of reaching out and asking for it.

Afterword

"He who conquers himself is greater than he who conquers a city"

Buddha

So you're at the end of the book. But in actual fact, you are at the beginning. Now it's the beginning of *your* journey. It's wonderful that you've read this far, but it's only in the 'doing' that we are able to make real transformations occur.

The proof, as they say, is in the pudding, so remember the key elements to success are self-discipline and consistency.

Putting our health first is the ultimate goal for our own wellbeing. Only when we do that can we be truly available for others. If you choose to put the actions outlined here into place and to work with the Innavision tools, you too can be the healthiest and the happiest you have ever been.

I wish you the very best of health.

Love,

Sandra

> *"One ounce of action is greater than one ton of theory"*
> *Ralph Waldo Emerson*

Online Resources

My website has weekly blogs / vlog and contains information on my services.
www.innavision.co.uk

Alcoholics Anonymous (AA)
http://www.alcoholics-anonymous.org.uk/

Food Addicts in Recovery Anonymous (FA)
http://www.foodaddicts.org/

NHS webpage mindfulness
http://www.nhs.uk/Conditions/stress-anxiety-depression/Pages/mindfulness.aspx

NHS webpage with tips on time management
http://www.nhs.uk/conditions/stress-anxiety-depression/pages/time-management-tips.aspx

Further Reading

There are many thousands of self-help books out there but these are two which were pivotal to my journey.

The Slight Edge by Jeff Olson
This book talks about a way of thinking and of processing information that enables you to make the daily choices that will lead you to success and happiness.

The Power of Now by Eckart Tolle
Eckhart Tolle demonstrates in this book how to live a healthier and happier life by living in the present moment.

ACKNOWLEDGEMENTS

Many thanks to Richenda who was there to make it happen. Grateful thanks go to my mentor Leo, my coach and dear friend who believed in me.

ABOUT THE AUTHOR

Sandra Crathern was born in 1960 in West Sussex. Having experienced many challenges in her own life which she worked hard to overcome, she now works with others to achieve the same. She is a Registered Nurse, an NLP Master Practitioner, and an ACC Accredited Life Coach.

This is her first book.

Sandra can be found at www.innavision.co.uk

Made in the USA
Charleston, SC
27 May 2016